Losing Our Religion

Exploring The Deconstruction of Christianity

RUTH EMBERY

Losing Our Religion: Exploring the Deconstruction of Christianity
Copyright © 2025 Ruth Embery
All rights reserved. No part of this publication may be reproduced, stored in, or introduced into a retrieval system, or transmittted, in any form, or by any means (electronic, mechanical, photocopying, recording or otherwise) without the prior written permission of the publisher.
Published by: Voice in the Dark Publishing
ISBN: 978-0-6453488-6-6 (Print)
ISBN: 978-0-6453488-7-3 (Electronic)

Unless otherwise noted, all scriptures are from THE HOLY BIBLE, NEW INTERNATIONAL VERSION®. Copyright© 1973, 1978, 1984, 2011 by Biblica, Inc.™. Used by permission of Zondervan

Scripture quotations marked AMP are taken from the Amplified® Bible, Copyright © 1954, 1958, 1962, 1964, 1965, 1987 by The Lockman Foundation. Used by permission. (www.Lockman.org)

Scripture quotations marked (CJB) are taken from the COMPLETE JEWISH BIBLE, Copyright© 1998 by David H. Stern. Published by Jewish New Testament Publications, Inc. www.messianicjewish.net. Distributed by Messianic Jewish Resources Int'l. www.messianicjewish.net. All rights reserved. Used by permission.

Scripture quotations marked (ESV) are taken from THE HOLY BIBLE, ENGLISH STANDARD VERSION®, Copyright© 2001 by Crossway, a publishing ministry of Good News Publishers. Used by permission.

Cover artwork © Ruth Embery

DEDICATION

To all on this journey - may you know the Spirit of Jesus, who is the Christ, as your ever-present guide.

Contents

Introduction	9
What's Your Metanarrative?	13
Minding Our Language	21
What Do You Mean You're Deconstructing?	25
Why Would Anyone Want to Deconstruct?	29
What's My Story?	35
What Do We Do About Unity?	41
About Judgement and Condemnation	47
What is the Word of God?	53
Worship and Prayer	57
What is Church?	67
Are You Saved?	75
What About Hell?	83
Conclusion	87
Who is Ruth Embery?	89
Appendix	91

ACKNOWLEDGEMENTS

As always, I would be remiss not to mention - and thank - my dear husband, Martin, without whom I may no longer be sane. He endeavours to keep me grounded and with my eyes on the main thing, and (generally) puts up with my endless iterations and revamps. I quite possibly single-handedly help him develop his patience muscle at times. His encouragement and endorsement of my enterprises are invaluable. I would also like to acknowledge his time in reading through most of this manuscript in the short amount of time I gave him!

I would also like to thank my friends, with a special mention to the Wednesday ladies, who accept me as I am, as well as encouraging, affirming and loving me so well. Thank you for coming on this part of the journey with me.

Secretly, my appreciation goes out to my lovely daughter as well, who loaned her photography skills and camera for the cover. She showed great patience and discernment, understanding what I wanted even when I couldn't explain it well and getting me some great shots to choose from.

And , of course, it almost goes without saying, I would not have put this book together without Jesus as my guide and stay. He knew what I needed before I had any idea, provided experiences, information and skills that have been invaluable. With Him beside me, the journey only ever gets more amazing!

Introduction

From my observations, the very idea of the deconstruction of Christianity seems to have many people either running in fear or coming out fighting in anger. A prevalent belief appears to be that those deconstructing are tossing out everything once held sacred and walking away from their faith. For many, it appears to be just another division in the Body of Christ. I would suggest, though, that the process of deconstructing has been going on within the wider church for many decades as we have struggled to stem the tide of the decline in numbers of those professing Christian faith. We just haven't labelled it as such.

As we unpack the various positions people take on the idea of deconstruction, some are holding fast to the security in their surety of all they have known in the past, while others are finding new freedom in permission to ask, to seek and to knock on the doors of many a sacred cow. Others are somewhere in between, or even totally unaware of the conversation.

Of course, it is understandably unsettling when what we thought we could take for granted no longer seems to hold water. When beliefs are leaking out for some, so is faith. If I don't believe x and y, then can I still be certain of z?

We also need to appreciate that numbers of people "deconstructing" have come out of situations of abuse (emotional and spiritual as well as financial and physical/sexual), seeing hypocrisy, lies, hurt and deception to varying levels, whether directed at them personally, or simply through observing what is going on within church communities. It is usually a very painful journey to walk away from all they have known, maybe for generations. Broken trust in any relationship, but even more so within a community, leaves us trying to discern anew what is true and what is not. If I can no longer trust pastors and leaders in their moral standards, can I trust them in anything, including what they have taught me about God and faith?

This journey is not only painful, but also can be quite traumatic. Perhaps we can liken it to going through an earthquake - are the foundations I have strong enough to carry me through and keep me safe? From a personal perspective, the forced deconstruction of my life expectations after the destruction of my marriage had an enormous impact on me at every level. Deconstructing faith has another level of intensity. There is loss of relationships, sometimes family as well as church family, loss of direction – which way is up? – and even loss of self and the relationship we may have thought we had with God. If these foundations are not true, what do I have left to stand on? The sense of overwhelm can be debilitating to say the least.

Perhaps some who are reading this introduction are already starting to feel the tendrils of offence or fear at even cracking open the door to the possibility of discussing these ideas. I ask your patience and trust to walk at least a little further down this path with me. Far from wanting to cause further division in writing this book, my barest hope is to create safe space for discussion and some openness toward understanding where others are heading.

Sadly, I have seen some heaping condemnation on those heading down the path of deconstruction and I wonder if they do not realise that they are simply compounding the problem? What those who are struggling actually require is a safe place where they can pull everything out a look at it through a new lens, reassess what to keep and what to throw out. For some, for sure, it can be tempting to throw everything out (the proverbial baby with the bath water), as they perceive it all as tainted with the pain and disappointment of their experiences.

For those feeling fearful or angry reading this, please stop and ask yourself what you are fearful of here? If your foundations of what you believe are strong, you will be confident in your answers for the questions I pose here. If you are fearful that some beliefs you have put your faith in are not true, can you trust God enough to keep you safe as you read on? The understanding that perfect love casts out all fear means that we don't need to worry about anything!

In the past, those in leadership have generally told us (as Christians) what to believe, and at times, we have agreed simply as part of gaining acceptance, whether we are aware of this or not. Perhaps we have observed the rejection of those who think differently or question the status quo, and realised it is not safe to do so, retreating back to silence as our protection. I know that has been part of my journey. I had a number of occurrences where those I thought were tracking with me and would support me, simply left me hanging out to dry when I questioned some things going on within church communities I have been involved in. Personally, I wonder if sometimes we don't switch off our ability to critically think or discern at the door of the church building in a (deeply hidden, perhaps) belief that it will keep us safe.

In the past, our inability to have mature and frank discussion to work through our issues and disagreements has been a major factor leading to the many denominations and factions we now see and the disunity in the Body of Christ, His Church. As much as unity is a very real passion to me, however, this book is not about how to restore unity. There is a distinct possibility, though, that reinvestigating the core message of Jesus may lead us once more down that path.

My prayer is that, at the very least, we can have greater compassion and grace for each other in this season, and respond in love, without demonising those we can't agree with.

What's Your Metanarrative?

Who do you listen to? Who is telling the narrative? What is their true driver?

We all have core beliefs and understanding of how the world and life works. Some of these are helpful, some not so much. The problem is, most of us are not even aware of these beliefs and understandings, let alone able to articulate them. Some we learnt generationally, others through schooling and societal or cultural norms. Much of the time, these inform what we believe is truth.[1]

In the past few decades, the concept of metanarratives has become more widely used. In a nutshell, understanding our metanarrative means to unpack the story or belief systems that form the foundations of our society, culture or sub-cultures.

Our metanarrative is what informs the stories we believe about ourselves, our culture, and the world. We have built everything we believe and value onto these foundations. A major problem occurs, however, when we don't understand the why or see the

---

[1] For more discussion on what truth is, see my book "Untruth: Exploring Truth in a Post-Truth World"

overall picture, or perhaps even agree with those foundations any more. Our behaviour will then gradually cease reflecting what we say we value and believe. I may get repetitive on this, but we find a far more insightful view of our values and beliefs illustrated by our behaviours. Or, to flip it, *our behaviour will illustrate or inform us of what we really believe and value.*

In the past, in the West particularly, the Church has been front and centre in telling us what to believe and to a lesser extent, why. With the increase in education over the last century or more, as more people learnt to read, as well as gaining increasing levels of critical awareness, many started to see holes, (either real or perceived), in the narrative the Church has provided. As this has often coincided with a lack of space for open and honest discussion, it has increasingly led to either new denominations or people simply leaving Christianity. (I am aware this is nowhere near the whole picture, but it is certainly one aspect.)

The discussion around what our metanarrative is, alongside the questions of who we will choose to believe and who we deem trustworthy has risen out of this shifting landscape of our culture and society.

An illustration of how far we have ventured down this path of questioning everything - or not questioning anything - came to the forefront for me (and many others) early on in 2020. As we grappled to come to terms with what was going on around us at a global level, the phrase "Experts are saying" became the precursor to many news reports. Trouble soon arose, however, as people became aware that not all experts were in agreement, and furthermore, not all experts were equally valued or given a voice. A fact many observed was that those experts who didn't toe the accepted line quickly found themselves dismissed as quacks or silenced in other ways.

As someone with a substantial background in the sciences (including a Bachelor of Science, with majors in chemistry and psychology), I too was more than a little sceptical. One of the key warnings lecturers gave us as we studied back in the 1980s was to recognise the impact underlying assumptions could make on the way we observed or interpreted results, as well as how easy it is to manipulate statistics to say what you would like. It was into this space that I wrote a post that friends on both sides of the fence could agree with, funnily enough both thinking I was supporting their view.

You can read the entirety of my tongue-in-cheek reflections and questions in Appendix 1. I wrote it as a prompt to try to encourage people to think about whether we are falling into a trap of simply accepting what we are told without further thought or any analysis. You might like to stop and actually reflect on your response to the following key questions from this post before you continue.

How do you choose your expert?

What do you mean, how do I choose my expert? An expert is an expert, aren't they? Or are some experts more expert than others? What makes someone an expert anyway? And who chooses who gets the title "expert"?

While these questions may appear rhetorical, they are an opportunity to move toward greater understanding.

The following are a few dot points on the topic:

- Just because some people are given the label expert doesn't mean they are an expert. We need to understand what they have actually done to become an expert, as well as who pays for their research. Most researchers are paid by organisations with a financial benefit from findings that support particular conclusions.

- Some of yesterday's experts are viewed as today's fools or have since been proven wrong (think flat earth, sugar vs fat in weight loss to name a couple).

- It is healthy for experts to express their disagreements with each other – robust conversation makes for outcomes we can have greater confidence in, that are more likely to stand the test of time.

- Many of today's narratives have an underlying agenda (acknowledged or not) to create division, money or both.

- You are allowed to ask questions, and anyone who tries to prevent you is probably either insecure or has another agenda.

As we step into unpacking a variety of beliefs built on assumptions and other beliefs, the idea of an expert is critically important. I have a number of friends and associates who are looking into what the Bible says about a variety of topics that seem relevant to this time for them. Often, I have heard words to the effect of, "this person is amazing, they know so much, they have been studying this for decades." This can be very intimidating when you start thinking differently. Who am I to come up against these "titans of the faith"?

As I mentioned earlier, the assumptions we build our beliefs on are very important. Most of us are not even aware that there are assumptions, let alone what they are. Often this is because we have been told theory or opinion as fact. And let's face it, there is a point at which we need to accept what someone else says, especially if we trust them. We don't all have the time, inclination or access to go to the same depth. However, there are times when we need to question the status quo, we need to dig a little deeper and maybe even in a different direction to find a better answer.

A couple of examples of the issues of wrong assumptions or foundations have come across my path recently. The latest was while watching a documentary of the building of a new underground train line in Rome.

In a city thousands of years old, as soon as you start digging, you are likely to find material of archaeological significance. In one such area, the archaeologists came and dug around, taking core samples in many areas down to a depth of five metres, which is where they expected any material of significance to be. Their conclusion was that there was nothing of importance to cause a problem, so the big diggers came in to start work on an underground station. That is, until they found something very significant…at nine metres down. This impacted the station site substantially. The point that was made is that sometimes we have to go further back in time to find what we are looking for.

The second example has to do with similar wrong assumptions. A few hundred years back when humans were starting to explore the last frontiers of earth (after they had gotten over their fear of falling off the edge of the flat earth – well really, to prove the inaccuracy of that belief, in many ways), there were certain places people went looking for what they felt sure should be there. Australia was one of those places they did find. Sometimes, however, they didn't find what they expected.

We were reminded of one of those situations, while we were travelling in outback New South Wales recently. Back in 1844, the well-known explorer, Charles Sturt, was convinced that in a land mass the size of Australia there must be an inland sea. So deep was his conviction that he carried a whaling boat, (on an oxen cart), from Adelaide in South Australia some 1500 kilometres through desert and heat before giving up and leaving the boat in far north New South Wales. His certainty was based on assumptions he made from his observations of bird behaviour among other ideas, but he was wrong and at great cost. A number of members of his team died and others became extremely unwell. He was so sure of his convictions, however, that he continued his search even while he was on the brink of death himself.

This leads to a third example which comes from the same trip. As we headed further out from populated areas, we had to rely more on the GPS system in the car for directions. Even in numbers of the towns we visited, our phones had no coverage, and of course, we had no hard copy maps. (Rookie mistake!)

There were a number of times as we drove that the mapping system in the car was woefully out of date. At one point we were on a major highway that we both knew was at least twenty years old, but the car map showed us as driving off road with no sign of the highway, and often told us to turn off at non-existent junctions. One reason for this issue is to do with Australia coming into line with other global systems as recently as 2020, as older systems were out of alignment. There is also the apparent fact that Australia is actually moving some seven centimetres to the north east each year, due to continental drift. This means that maps using GPS for location constantly require updating.

The point with this is that if we build on a foundation that is even a tiny bit out of alignment, or based on a wrong assumption at some level, by the time we get some way along the course, we find that we are a long way off base of where we thought we were going. If we are just a little out of kilter in our foundational beliefs, the resulting impact on our behaviour can be immense. If we are missing pertinent information because we haven't gone back far enough, or deep enough, our assumptions may be significantly off base.

Over the past 2000 years, it is easy to understand that a tiny creep off course may have impacted our understanding way more than we realise. Conversely, we do have increasing awareness and appreciation of the massive cultural shifts over those millennia and how they have impacted our beliefs. In the past, we have often failed to consider the underlying beliefs of Jewish culture in our understanding of scripture. This has led to many incorrect assumptions and beliefs, not to mention missing out on a greater depth and wealth of meaning. As we become more aware of these factors, it opens the door to reassess a number of our views.

Minding Our Language

"You keep using that word. I do not think it means what you think it means."[2]

"When meaning is torn from words, life is drained of its substance and the world is transformed into a wasteland."[3]

One of the most important aspects of any conversation is understanding what we actually mean by the language we use. Our communication can be severely hampered when we have even the slightest differences in how we interpret the words used, not to mention tone and body language. Our experiences within the topic being discussed will also colour the way we comprehend what we hear.

While this might seem obvious, we don't always take into account the way in which culture and beliefs can impact nuances of meaning in words. Further, over time, some words have overtly been transposed into a completely new meaning. Unless we are on the same page with those we talk with, this

---
2 Inigo Montoya, "The Princess Bride"
3 David Patterson, in "Hebrew Language and Jewish Thought".

can easily lead to dissension and disconnection. If you have connected with teens at any point, you will be aware of cultural language that sometimes has no meaning to others. It actually becomes a separate language, creating even more of a division in understanding. IYKYK. (If you know, you know.)

Having travelled to a few different countries, I am also aware of the fact that even though we both might speak English, we may have very different interpretations of some words and concepts. One that readily comes to mind is in Indonesia, where a person will not say "No" to a request, but rather, when they say "Maybe", that actually means no.

Further, there are times words are used as labels to create division and hatred. A word that gets a work out in the Australian political arena is to claim certain people or behaviours are "unAustralian". What exactly does that mean? What does it mean to be Australian? When we use words to demonise or otherwise destroy people's identity, it is heartbreaking at the least.

Over the last couple of decades, many of us have deliberated the concept of "Christian-ese", particularly around the impact it has on the increasing numbers of people with little or no church background. Unfortunately, so much of this type of language still gets used in social media posts and the like, and even more unfortunately, often as a stick of condemnation to beat up those who may think differently to the post-writer.

In reality, while being perhaps some sort of shorthand - a word to describe something much more complex and nuanced – I believe many of these "Christian" words actually become divisive, creating and gulf between those who get it and those who don't. This has the potential to leave people feeling as though they are not good enough, stupid or bad because they really don't understand what the words mean. Otherwise, they simply pretend they do, taking on board implications that leave them stuck, far from giving them the freedom Jesus promises.

Personally, I find many of these words have become meaningless. In addition, what are the other assumptions tagged to them and where do they lead us? For example, what are we redeemed or saved from, and if we have been saved, why do we still behave as though we need to work harder at being worthy or accepted? What does it mean to be righteous and how do we talk about this without it appearing to condemn everyone who is not on the same path as us?

Sadly, it reminds me of the teachers of the law and the Pharisees, who Jesus censured about how they presented the law as opposed to how they enacted it. He acknowledged the pain the common people were feeling from how these teachers taught, saying, *"They tie up heavy, cumbersome loads and put them on other people's shoulders, but they themselves are not willing to lift a finger to move them."* (Matt 23:4).

If we reflect on how Jesus taught, although the scriptures tell us that He taught with authority, He also used parables and familiar concepts from the everyday life of His listeners. They didn't need to understand complex terms and religious language to understand what He was talking about. They got it immediately and clearly.

One of the major issues I see with using religious language is that it continues to create a divide between *us* and *them*, or those who went to Bible College, those who have studied Greek and Hebrew and the uneducated general populace. It creates a hierarchy and an inner sanctum of those at the top as opposed to all the other church-goers. I have personally heard and witnessed these attitudes and beliefs. They often come packaged with a level of arrogance, given the education levels of many congregation members, not to mention the value of their life experiences. These attitudes usually come with a dismissal of the ability of those sitting in the pews to hear anything of value or import from God for themselves.

Lately, there has been something of a shift in this perspective as numbers of leaders have started to talk about church as family. Although the language may have changed, however, by and large the hierarchy is still in place. This is an illustration of how we might try to change outward appearances, but without changing the underlying structures and beliefs, we are deceiving ourselves if we think it will lead to meaningful change.

The next few chapters will explore some of these terms and the issues they tend to create, with some hope to remove some of the disconnection and perhaps suggest a different way forward.

What Do You Mean You're Deconstructing?

Possibly the most important term to define is what those using it mean by the concept of deconstruction. Although this might seem oversimplified for some, spelling it out clearly hopefully alleviates the possibilities of misunderstanding.

Simply looking at the spelling, we can easily see the link between deconstruction and construction. Breaking it down (pun intended), to construct is to build something. A construction can refer to a building, or mean the assembling of something out of a variety of parts – whether it be a physical building, a computer, a book or a wedding cake. By definition, deconstruction is the opposite. It is the disassembling of the parts that make a whole.

While some might view this as destruction and thereby damaging, feeling it is possibly irreversible, we can learn much from any process of deconstruction.

I would liken it to building with LEGO®[4] bricks. We can build a structure using many differing parts of the kit. I can use all the

---

4 LEGO® is a trademark of the LEGO Group of companies which does not sponsor, authorize or endorse this work.

same pieces as you and build something that looks completely different and even has a different purpose.

We may believe that the purpose of the Church or the Body of Christ is obvious and believed by any true Christian. When we observe at the activities and expectations within individual church communities, though, it is very clear – often painfully so – that even the stated purpose or mission statement may not get a look in much of the time.

The process of deconstruction enables us to investigate the varying aspects of what we call Christianity – how they come together, what is important/vital, what is not. We can see how the parts function, and may even find parts that inhibit the working of the whole or work against each other.

As a further example of some of the issues of this process, the concept of a deconstructed meal is something that has popped up in the past decade or so. To create something new or inspiring, I assume, someone decided to start presenting food with its individual components separated out. The sceptic in me wonders whether someone half dropped a plate at some point, but they had run out of the main ingredient, so thought of a new term to describe a mess. It is not a mess, simply deconstructed!

A great illustration of a deconstructed meal could be a "deconstructed burger", where the bun, lettuce, tomato, cheese, onions, patty and pickles are all placed separately on the plate. It shows us exactly what is in there and possibly, how they go together. No doubt, though, there are those who believe that it ceases to be a burger if it is not all placed together as I envision (or like) my burger presented to me.

Of course, there are also those who are happy to argue with each other about what actually constitutes a burger – what are the essential ingredients? A friend noted that for those in the USA, a burger with a piece of chicken instead of a beef patty is not a burger. Others would say if it doesn't have beetroot (an Australian favourite) it is not a burger, or you can't add pineapple. The type of cheese, sauce and mayonnaise are further examples of what various people see as essential to make these ingredients into a burger. In fact, there was a joke going around about a patron of a certain global burger store using the "select your own" option, and removing so much that it was basically some lettuce and tomato. At just what point is it no longer a burger? Exactly what are the crucial ingredients?

Can you imagine a scenario where we possibly come to any sort of agreement about what these crucial components are for a burger? There are so many influencing factors for each of us, from what we enjoy to what we grew up with to what others and experience have taught us about everything a burger should be. More recently, it will now include what our digestive tolerances are!

If we superimpose these thoughts over the idea of deconstructing Christianity, the starting point of deconstruction can certainly just look like a mess. For some, undoubtedly, this mess is so overwhelming, and the loss of the surety and security around the structure they used to know is so intense and scary that they feel they must abandon the journey or maybe just slam the door on any further discussion.

Initially, we can start the discussion around what is essential to being a Christian, whatever that means either to me, to those in my circle, or to the community I live within. I know I am not alone in wondering whether "Christian" is even helpful nomenclature anymore, given the bad rap Christianity has been given over the past few decades. In fact, I have a number of personal connections who have a very dim view of anyone who claims to be Christian. Even though they have known me for a long time, they now view me and everything I do through that lens.

In the light of these issues, any agreement on what the essential facets of the Christian faith are seems like smoke in the wind. Just like what is essential in a burger. Is it possible to nail it down?

Unfortunately, people from all walks of life have debated on - and failed to come to agreement on - what makes someone a Christian and who should be in and who should be out ad nauseum for hundreds of years. This is a major reason why we have so much division, dissension and denominations in the so-called Body of Christ. Is there still hope?

Bringing it in closer again, in our personal (and wider) pride, each group is certain that they have it more correct than the other group down the road or across the street. Perhaps the closer the physical proximity to us, the more wrong the others are? Because, just maybe, if they have it right too, we might need to lower our fences, get out of our ivory towers (or black boxes), step out of our comfort and connect with them more readily. But then, if we can be in agreement with them, why do we need the separation of space? And then, if I'm being really cynical, who gets to be the head? (Ouch!)

Why Would Anyone Want to Deconstruct?

When looking at statistics around church membership, attendance and those calling themselves Christian, there is little room for doubt that the Western church as we have known it has been in quite dire straits for some time. For several decades now, people have been leaving what they have seen as church in droves. Covid-19 only seemed to exacerbate the flood of the departing.

Even though many of these people are completely leaving their faith behind as irrelevant, a good proportion of those exiting the institutional church are actually in the process of deconstructing their faith, reassessing what is central and important. This reassessment was something that many of us did in a variety of ways during our seasons of being locked down in 2020 and 2021. In fact, I would suggest that, as we have been involved in discussions looking at the way forward for the church, a large number of us have been deconstructing for decades. We just didn't label it as such.

While those in a wide array of circles have acknowledged and discussed the issue of people leaving, especially in the higher echelons of leadership of various denominations and church groups, it would appear that little of their efforts have made much difference. From the ideas of looking to make church more relevant and more culturally accessible, to using business models to try to keep the financials afloat, little seems to have made much impact on stemming the tide of exodus in many church communities.

I have my own ideas about what some problems are, and I am aware that numbers of other people share many of those thoughts. However, these people tend to be those on the edges or even outside what we generally call the church. Conversely, it appears that many in the centre are still trying to hold on to their positions (whether that is in leadership, or in traditions of faith), while trying to reinvent the wheel.

In fact, I believe that a dream I had some years back now relates directly to this. In the dream, I was in the observation room of a surgical theatre. In this large white room was a rather rotund white/pink man on a table with a number of doctors and experts around him. As the dream unfolded, he started screaming in pain and I became aware that he was trying to give birth. While immediately thinking how unnatural it was for a man to give birth, simultaneously, I was thinking that might be what we should expect in the current climate. One of the major issues of this birthing scenario, however, was the lack of adequate body parts for the baby to come out through.

The doctors were also realising this, and (yes, my dream was really this gruesome), turning the man over, they started to cut him open from the buttocks up his back. As they did, they were removing his skin, and there was the thought (discussion?) about the idea that he would need a new skin. I was suddenly aware of a dark-skinned man standing to the side, and there was a sense that they were going to use this man's skin as a replacement. At that point, I had had enough and woke up.

As I pondered the meaning of this dream, I really sensed that it was a picture of the machinations of many in the church, trying desperately to birth something new, but all they have really been doing is putting a different colour of paint on the walls, whether literally or figuratively. (Although it is interesting that many churches have been going down the path of painting the inside walls of their auditoriums black over the past decade or so.)

While we continue to try to do something new without digging more deeply into our true underlying beliefs and perceptions, our metanarrative, we are destined to keep going around the same hamster wheel. The view may appear different, but the outcome is the same.

If we really want to improve outcomes and reassess our operations, both personally and corporately, a helpful process here can be the five[5] or seven[6] layers of why.

The principle is to repeatedly ask "Why?" around each aspect of what we do or believe in order to get to our deeper beliefs. It also helps us to identify the true problem we are trying to solve, rather than just dealing with the symptoms. This is a great tool to work out why what we do is not working the way we think it should, as well as helping us to find better ways to achieve the outcome we really want.

---

5   Sakichi Toyoda
6   Joe Stump

An example of how this works could be related to church attendance. Our belief or desire may be that we need to get people back into church. We ask the question, "Why?" Our answer may be, "Because we must not give up meeting together."

"Why?"

"Because the Bible says so."

"Why?"

"Because it is helpful to us."

"Why?"

"Because we can encourage and support each other."

"Why?"

"So people don't fall away from faith."

"Why (is that a problem for us)?"

You may have different answers to these questions and you may or may not agree with the answers given. The last question will really begin to get to what the core belief is, and hopefully identify the passion of the leadership, if they answer truthfully. It may be "Because we will have less people in our congregation and less finances, and I might be out of a job…"

As I have observed church communities trying to change, a problem I see is that we often just seem to keep trying to change our image or exterior appearance (be that the building or the way we do things around the place). Inherent problems that have built up in the last generation or two, or maybe centuries are not addressed at all, however.

Certainly, some of the changes that have impacted the wider Church have been external, at a cultural or global level. However, many of these external changes and attitudes have arisen because of distortions rather than a true portrayal of Christianity. As we continue, I will unpack some of these and even to make some suggestions of what might need to change. I will share largely from my own journey - my questions, observations and discoveries, so it may be somewhat anecdotal. However, there is, as always, the invitation to taste and see for yourself.

What's My Story?

My faith journey began in earnest in my teens, back in the early 1980s. There are many aspects about this time that make more sense to me now, especially understanding what was going on at a global level within a number of facets of the Christian faith. This included sudden growing numbers of people deciding to follow Jesus, particularly coming out of the drug and hippy scene. These people were truly seeking, after throwing out much of what previous generations had believed and how they had lived. They saw a great deal of hypocrisy and a lack of freedom in the status quo of society at that time. From the reports of many of these people, they found something very real in Jesus. However, within this outbreak, the traditional church had some understandings, beliefs and expectations that were not always helpful.

While many in mainstream Christianity did work hard to adapt to accept these new believers, eventually those changes either became part of the mainstream, proved ineffectual, or were maybe a bit of both. (The Jesus Revolution movie very clearly illustrates some of what was going on back then.)

Personally, I grew up in the church scene, with members of both my family lines invested deeply in their faith, way beyond nominal Christianity. My mother's grandparents were missionaries in far north India (now Pakistan). They left England in 1902 about a week after getting married, in a time when travel was extremely slow and difficult, as were communications. This couple had nine children and literally lived out their faith. Their children reflected that sometimes they would not know where their next meal would come from, how their needs would be met, but never remember going hungry. Food or money would turn up when they needed it from a wide variety of sources, whether they were local (and not necessarily people of the same faith) or from their supporters back in England. My great-grandfather set out with what he deeply believed was a very clear call to go where he went, especially given that other mission agencies and the wider church did not support him at all.

My father's parents left Adelaide, Australia to minister in a church in London, back in the early 1930s. When the second world war broke out, they wrestled with whether to return to Australia or to stay. They ended up staying, but at quite a sacrifice on many levels. My grandmother took the children to live just outside London, while my grandfather felt compelled to stay to support and encourage those remaining in Islington where they were based. There were many times they didn't know whether he had survived the many bombings, and indeed, we have letters between them describing how harrowing some of those times were, including a bomb landing only a few houses away from their home. Their letters from that time reveal a very real reliance on their faith.

These people had a deep faith and deep convictions to be able to do what they did, and I believe my parents operated out of much the same faith, especially earlier on in their lives. However, as I was growing up, God did not seem hugely personal. In fact, the idea of a personal God, a personal relationship with Him was not something we discussed. We talked a lot about theology and how we were to understand God, as well as quite a lot about how to be a better Christian (whatever that might mean – very much behaviourally based), but I had no real grid for a relationship with God. In fact, mostly it left me feeling He was someone too perfect, too mighty and too far away, while I was a mere nobody. The separation between our faith life and secular life was also growing.

Enter the 1980s. I went to a Christian secondary school, and in that space, connected with a number of people with some different beliefs about what it meant to be Christian. At that time, one of the most significant ideas was exactly around this idea of a personal relationship with God and the idea of accepting Jesus as your personal Lord and Saviour. While I don't reject this idea in its essence, it came with a few qualifications that I struggled with for years and still find myself coming up against today.

While my purpose in this book is not to debunk certain theologies, I would like to pull a few out and reinvestigate them. This will especially focus on the issues and struggles these views create for numerous followers of Jesus, as well as the fear, condemnation and bondage that tend to become attached to these perceptions.

Personally, even as the concept of a relationship with God opened up a whole other facet of faith to me, a couple of teachings that came with it also created a huge struggle for me. Was I good enough? Was I accepted? One of the main preaching tools (that still remains in many circles today) was using the question, "If you died tonight, would you go to heaven or hell?" I am well aware, that for some, that question may be triggering you right now! Either you still haven't come to terms with it (Am I in or not? Is it permanent? What about those sins last week, yesterday, years ago? How can I be sure?), or perhaps you have been trying to break free of the fear that is associated with that idea. Or you may just be angry with the people who held that as a weapon over your head, or the heads of those you love. We will delve deeper into this further on.

The other very prevalent teaching was around the book of Revelation, along with a movie called, "Thief in the Night". This movie explored the idea of Jesus returning, taking all the "true believers" and everyone else being "left behind" to face the horrors of the apocalypse. As a young teen, I had a number of nightmares about these sorts of scenarios, interspersed with the other fear of that age – nuclear war. In fact, this was one of the first really obvious answers to prayer that I had, asking Jesus to stop those nightmares. (And they instantaneously ceased!)

Partly because of the era I grew up in (question everything!), and partly because I grew up in a family that valued independent thought and understanding, as the years went by I began on something of a quest to have a deeper grasp of the faith I had grown up in and professed.

In my early twenties, as I read Acts, the main question I had was, "Why don't we see all this today?" The perception of Christianity taught in the churches and groups I attended seemed to have very little in common with what the early disciples experienced. I was hungry for something more, but had little idea what it actually might look like.

Another question I had concurrently with these thoughts about church was around how we could hear from God for the important decisions of life, such as career and marriage. Those around me didn't seem to move far from the standard response of "Read your Bible more", and "Pray more". Mostly I felt as though I was fumbling about in very dim light, hoping I was heading in the right direction, and that if I was wrong, somehow God would put up a stop sign. Looking back, my connection to God was very tenuous and fragile at best.

This journey was important and has definitely led me to where I am today and even to writing this book. I am including it, however, to explain the background of what I see as a major issue and major flaw in how many of us view our faith. Hopefully it also explains why I am so passionate about these issues.

What Do We Do About Unity?

Back around 2017, I found myself continually drawn to John 17 – the longest recorded prayer of Jesus. In the middle of this (verses 20-23), Jesus prays that all His followers would be one, just as He and the Father are one. I don't know about you, but I struggle to find that level of oneness with people I mostly agree with. What a big call! As I reflected on this passage, it seemed very clear to me that this prayer of Jesus is recorded because He knew it would be one of our biggest struggles. It is something so difficult, especially with the mindsets most of us operate out of around the concept of unity.

The major issue we have with unity is defining what it is, what do we mean by being united or in unity?

One pastor I spoke to about local church communities working together actually said to me that his congregation would not do anything collaborative with other groups if they didn't believe certain things. (He failed to express what those things were though.)

Again, this is not a new conversation. Interestingly (especially to me), as I was doing some research on my paternal grandfather,

I found a document he and a number of other Melbourne ministers produced way back in 1958. It was the very beginning of discussions that led to the Uniting Church in Australia coming into being. (I remember back at the time of the launch in 1977 that they explained the name saying that it wasn't "united" but "uniting" as they hoped and looked forward to other denominations joining in. Sadly, the Uniting Church appears on such a steep decline that it will soon cease to exist without some sort of miraculous turn around. But I digress.)

What was interesting to me in my research, however, was the explainer at the beginning of this 1958 document. The foundation of this fledgling movement between Presbyterians, Methodists and Congregationalists was not based on everyone believing all the same about everything. Rather, they started by listing *all the aspects of faith they could agree on*. This was their "collective belief". Perhaps this is the starting point for further movements toward some sort of unity. Start with the question, *"What can we agree on?"*

Personally, as I think about what precepts should be at the base of any sort of unity, I can't help but return to who Jesus is and the only real commands He gave us. Love God with all your heart, mind and soul. Love one another as I have loved you.

As much as we all give hearty assent to this (after all, are any of us willing to go head-to-head with Jesus on this one?), the reality is that every person on this planet struggles to love at least some people some of the time. It never ceases to amaze me, though, how many people who would identify as Christians on various forums can speak so horribly about people they disagree with or have been in some way hurt by. Then there are those describing various Christian leaders as being of the devil, evil and so on.

I don't think Jesus gave us the option of behaving in unloving ways to anyone. He pretty much nailed it with "love your enemies". (Matt 5:44-45). "But I tell you, love your enemies and pray for those who persecute you, that you may be children of your Father in heaven. He causes his sun to rise on the evil and the good, and sends rain on the righteous and the unrighteous."

Of course, we also need to be clear on what love looks like. It is not just being nice, not just doing what the other person wants to make them happy. Sometimes it looks like saying no, or not engaging in otherwise unhelpful behaviour. In addition, if Jesus has called us to love one another as ourselves, and we have no love for ourself, then it is very difficult to love others. And we can only love ourselves as we experience the love of the Father.

When we put the ideas presented in 1 John 4 about no one having the capacity to love without experiencing the love of God, alongside these two commandments, it becomes plain to me. The level to which we have experienced the love of God in every aspect of our being (especially all the dark and painfilled spaces we'd rather not think about), is the level to which we can start to love others. I would go so far as to suggest that the ways in which we are unloving to others is where we are also unloving to ourselves. It is worth thinking about. What I hate about myself, I work hard to expunge in the world around me, not realising I need to start internally. By bringing that aspect of myself to Jesus and receiving the healing balm of His love, it reduces or changes the impact that seeing the same behaviour, attitude or belief in others has on me. I can have greater compassion on others. But that is for another book.

I don't have the answers to how we do unity. I do believe it comes back to one of my favourite quotes from "The Shack", by William

P Young. The chief protagonist, Mack, is talking with Sophia (Wisdom), who, after a very confronting discussion, exclaims to him, "You have judged them [his children] to be worthy of love".

We are told in Rom 5:8, "But God demonstrates His love for us in this: While we were still sinners, Christ died for us." We had done, and can do, nothing to deserve Jesus' gift of His love. Why do we have greater expectations for others, that they should behave in certain ways before they are worthy of our love, or even respect?

One of the major reasons, in my belief system, is to do with the Garden of Eden and what happened there. Reading "There Were Two Trees in the Garden", by Rick Joyner many years back was a real game changer for me. It gave me language for what I had been sensing and struggling with within the church as I experienced it.

Joyner describes the two trees as representing two kingdoms, picking up on Jesus' language, so often referring to the Kingdom of God or Kingdom of Light in contrast to the kingdom of darkness. Genesis 2:9 introduces us to the tree of life and the tree of the knowledge of good and evil. In his discussion, Joyner describes the second tree as two sides of the same coin, neither of which lead to life. When we operate from this tree, we are constantly having to sit in judgement over what, (or who) is right and what, (or who) is wrong. This creates constant and ever-increasing division between who is good enough and who is not.

Jamie Winship (co-creator of the Identity Exchange) also talks a great deal about the two kingdoms, but refers to them as the kingdoms of separation and connectedness.

Unfortunately, much of the language used within church circles lends itself far more to the tree of the knowledge of good and evil, and separation than to bringing life, freedom and connectedness. This segues very nicely into the next section.

About Judgement and Condemnation

Early in my healing journey, for a period of time, Romans 8:1 was my mantra. Every time I was feeling condemned and bad about myself, I would say it out loud. "Therefore, there is no condemnation for those in Christ Jesus". I like the Complete Jewish Bible version even better, now: "Therefore, there is no longer any condemnation for those who are in union with the Messiah Yeshua."

When we understand our unity with Jesus, we can live free from the condemnation the world would heap on us and we often heap on ourselves. As we further unpack the concept of being in unity with Jesus, however, it makes me wonder how we can believe that we are in union with Jesus, but deliver the verdict that others are not? Logic would tell me that if I am in union with God and you are in union with God, then for me to refuse to be in unity with you requires some sort of disconnect – both of us must only partially be in union with God for that to happen. Where is that separation coming from? As I have suggested earlier, if I refuse to be in unity with others, it is usually because I have made the decision that they are not right or good enough.

And, of course, this presents another problem. Do I actually believe I can be in unity with Jesus? Do I really believe I am good enough? And what does being in unity actually mean? Do I have to give up everything that I hold dear and go to be a missionary in some far-flung impoverished country to be worthy of true unity? If we are not sure we want to do everything we believe Jesus would ask of us if we were truly in union with Him, it is way safer for us to keep a little distance, a little separation from Him.

In Jamie Winship's teaching, he refers to us operating out of the place of scarcity or lack. If I believe that there is not enough (to satisfy my needs/wants), or I am not enough, or you are not enough in some way, I believe there is something lacking. To overcome this lack, I can either work harder or make you work harder. It leads to perfectionism, competition and comparison, jealousy, the need for control and certainty, fear, and ultimately, we live in the place of separation. Sound familiar?

When we live from a place of connection with God, we no longer have expectations of others or ourselves to fill any lack. We can live from the place of fullness and embrace the mystery of not having to know or control. It is a place where mistakes are opportunities to learn, rather than failings and we can connect with others from a place of interdependence which leads to community – or "common unity" – where we give and take without expectations because we already know we are enough and there is enough. We can be generous with each other materially, emotionally and with grace because we are convinced that there is always enough.

We can unpack a great deal more from these thoughts, particularly around why we don't engage with this way of living. I believe the problem comes back to us having a fundamental distrust of God's goodness and being uncertain, at some deep level, of whether He is trustworthy.

We can't deal with our issues of feeling constantly condemned, however, without also talking about judgement. Unfortunately, somewhere along the line, these two words became synonymous. Anyone who makes any sort of judgement we dislike is immediately *judged* as being condemning, and we are generally totally unaware of the irony of our own judgement. (It reminds me of one of our social commentators some years back, proudly announcing that she was intolerant of people she deemed intolerant!) There is some level at which we have come to the belief that making any judgement about anything is bad. This word is in need of some serious restoration!

By definition judgement is actually related to making decisions. One description is "the ability to form valuable opinions and make good decisions."[7] From my observations, our culture has mostly stripped that meaning from the idea of judgement. As discussed earlier, it would appear that many of us have abdicated our responsibility to judge or make decisions for ourselves about anything we believe or observe. That being said, I am also aware of the pain of condemnation and rejection when others accuse us of being (negatively) judgemental, sometimes when we are only making an observation or asking a question. Perhaps we have developed an oversensitivity? Having seen overly harsh condemnation, has the pendulum swung so far in the other direction that now any discernment is taboo?

Unfortunately, the issue is closely connected to the way in which the concept of judgement has been taught to us from the Old Testament - that God will judge the evil doers so we better not

---

7   https://dictionary.cambridge.org/dictionary/english/judgment

be one, or even associate with one. Again, it ties into the tree of the knowledge of good and evil. This mindset keeps us in a constant cycle of needing to judge between what is good and what is not. And mostly, we don't realise how unqualified we are to do this, particularly in how it relates to what other people do. Generally, we have no idea about why they do what they do or what they are trying to survive.

More recently, Jesus has challenged me with how much I am still living my life out of this place of judging whether what others do is ok or not on so many levels. To put it in general terms, every time we talk about other people in terms of "They do this", or "They believe that", in any way observing whether or not we think they are doing something good, helpful or right, we are coming from that place of making our own decisions about their "goodness" or "badness". We believe we know and understand every nuance of why they are like that, and therefore can judge that they should know or do better.

In our understanding and reclaiming of the word judgement, replacing it with idea of discernment or deciding, instead of condemnation, may be a starting point. I also firmly believe that we need to stop assessing people we dislike or disagree with in any way in such a black and white manner. Based on one belief about someone, we decide whether they are good or bad, in or out, Christian or of the devil. The verdicts we make about others usually simply create further division and also tend to devalue them, not just in our eyes, but in the eyes of those we talk with.

When we talk about "them" and what "they" do or think or believe, we are creating an us and them – people I feel safe with, who think like me, and people who are not safe, who think differently. The reason this makes us feel safe, I would suggest, is that fundamentally we are not that sure of our own position or standing. We believe that forming these boundaries will make us safe. While there might seem some truth in that, we become very dependent on other people's opinion of us. Eventually they let us down or hurt us, and then we disconnect from them. In the long run, we wind ourselves ever more tightly inward in trying to control everything and everyone around us to keep us feeling safe. (Got a book on that one, too…[8])

Underlying the issue of the judgement that condemns others is legalism - our desire for laws and certainty to feel safe. In the context of community, we need to do this or that or believe this or that to be "in", to be ok. Otherwise, we are "out". While we may speak against any form of obvious legalism, we may still subtly operate from this same space. An inherent operating system within us sets up boundaries (to keep us safe) and that leads to a list of behaviours and beliefs that we deem acceptable.

In my reflections, I wonder if we use these boundaries as some sort of shorthand device? Rather than putting in the work to have relationship with people without preconceived ideas of who they are and what we will find out about them, we make rapid decisions about them to expedite our conclusion on whether this person is worth investing my valuable time in. And sometimes, we do this vicariously through someone else's opinion, with even less firsthand information.

Then there is another question doing the rounds: "Do you value being right over retaining a relationship?" The premise here is that often we will sacrifice relationship when we can't convince the other person that "I am right and you are wrong". We refuse to give space to the dissonance we feel if we can't convince the

---

[8] "Handing Back Control"

other person they are wrong. Instead of valuing the other person, we would rather just end the relationship and so, disconnect for our own comfort.

Underneath this behaviour, in my opinion, is deep insecurity. If I can't prove I am right, I am on shaky ground and feel like my foundations may crumble. Perhaps it is because we really don't trust God loves us in all our failings, we haven't experienced His grace toward us, so we have no grace to extend toward others?

What is the Word of God?

This idea leads to another question. What exactly are my foundations? We are probably all well aware of the lyrics of the old hymn, "on Christ the solid rock I stand, all other ground is sinking sand..."[9]. The idea of Jesus being our Rock, our foundation is one most Christians would adhere to, but what do we really mean when we say this? How is He our foundation and what are the characteristics of that foundation?

Immediately, this leads me to another of my pet frustrations with language used by many Christians. "I stand on the Word of God!" numerous people proclaim loudly, holding up their Bible.

Reading the Bible, labelled "The Word" by a vast majority leaves us with a rather awkward conflict. John 1:1, 10 states, "In the beginning was the Word, and the Word was with God, and the Word was God... He was in the world, and though the world was made through Him, the world did not recognize Him." I doubt any Christian would disagree that this was referring to Jesus. So why do a large proportion of us keep referring to the Bible as the Word and the only reference point?

---
9   Edward Mote: Public Domain

Although we might talk of having a relationship with Jesus through the Bible, and yes, it is a good starting point, it is quite impersonal. He did tell us that we would know and listen to His voice (John 10), which indicates a more intimate relationship than we can gain simply by reading about Him in a book that has been through much so much interpretive translation from a very different era that we have little understanding about. We may have a great deal of intellectual understanding, but what is our experience?

Of course, as soon as we open the can of worms around the Bible or scripture, we also need to address the argument of which translation is best or even correct. With little understanding of an ancient language, let alone the way in which translations are created, we cannot say definitively that anything is correct. A translator must decide which word is best within the context of the passage and this will be impacted by the assumptions and beliefs the translator comes with, not to mention any agenda of those paying for the translation. They also require a good grasp of the culture and issues that were going on at the time, rather than the lens of current culture. This is very difficult some 2000 years later. We need to be very careful of stating too categorically that any translation has got it all right.

This leads me to another way in which use of the Bible tends to be abused. A verse that often quoted with a distorted lens is 2 Tim 3:16, that all scripture is useful for teaching, rebuking, correcting and training. This verse is nearly always (as far as I can tell, anyway), used to include the whole of the Bible including the New Testament.

When we stop and think for only a minute, we must realise that Paul purportedly wrote these words some three to four hundred years before leaders decided to put together what they called the canon of scripture, the Bible, somewhat as we know it today, which then includes these letters. So, when we quote this verse, which portion of the Bible are we referring to? At best we can only refer to the material the Jewish people of that time referred to as Scripture, which included the Torah (the first five books), Nevi'im (The Prophets) and the Ketuvim (other writings). As many an atheist will tell you, there are numerous commands in this portion of Scripture most of us would never dream of obeying, including who to stone when. When we choose to ignore this dissonance, we not only do ourselves a disservice, but we also create huge hurdles for others to get over.

Worship and Prayer

Reflecting on the concepts of worship and prayer and whether they are actually important has been one of the more difficult and disturbing parts of my journey. I have been very passionate in both these areas for most of my adult life, including leading worship within the Sunday morning custom in a couple of seasons.

Through the last thirty something years, I have been involved in numerous discussions with various people about what constitutes worship. The heavy emphasis on worship as music and singing has created a bone of contention, particularly for those without musical backgrounds, those who don't enjoy engaging with music in that way, or those who have differing preferences for the style of music used.

As part of a variety of leadership teams, as we have unpacked a little more of what is meant by worship and how we might help those in our congregations to participate more adequately, a few things stand out for me. (Please note, plenty of books have focussed on this, so it is not my intent to create another dissertation.)

First, although music can be very helpful in creating an atmosphere and focus, in itself, music is not worship. By definition, worship is about the worth we designate to an object or person. One definition describes worship as: *"to honor or show reverence for as a divine being or supernatural power; to regard with great or extravagant respect, honor, or devotion"*[10] . The root of this word goes back to the idea of ascribing worth. We can do this in any number of ways, whether that be through song, through words spoken, but perhaps more importantly, our actions, attitudes and behaviours can be a great indicator of what we truly worship, and often, unfortunately, may not match up with what we sing or speak.

I believe this is one of the key areas in which many people have become disenfranchised with Christianity – particularly what they observe of it. Our worship can so easily become lip-service, something we do outwardly that really doesn't reflect what is going on internally. We come and do our duty to God, as we see it, and don't expect it to mean anything past some nice words or good feelings at best. For those not musically inclined, it can even be painful, causing them to feel as though they are at fault and not acceptable to God. In circles where only the chosen beautiful ones are up on the stage leading worship, our services have also often become more like a concert with an audience and performers than a cohesive community coming together.

As I have reflected on some of the patterns I have observed, particularly within the more Pentecostal or charismatic church communities, I myself have felt more and more disconnected from God in these spaces. What used to be my happy space, something that brought me joy and made me feel closer to God has become hard work and often filled with disappointment.

---

10   Merriam-Webster Dictionary: https://www.merriam-webster.com

Previously, I have felt it was something deficient in me, that I was not in a good place, or I was disconnecting from God because of some aspect of my being that needed healing. More recently, however, I have started to ask Him what is going on, and the answer that has landed makes sense.

There are two aspects that I have observed here. One is with worship leaders having an agenda. It is not necessarily a bad agenda, but the problem is that it can become manipulative. We want to see God move or manifest in some way. We want to see healings, or people weeping or laughing. Maybe we want to see gold dust and feathers falling. Unfortunately, at our depths, what we really want is for God to prove Himself to us. We want Him to reward us for our worship of Him with some outworking that is tangible to us.

More recently, observing a prayer and worship time (in another country), Queen Jezebel's prophets of Ba'al (1 Kings 18:20-40) kept coming to mind. In the story, they keep getting their fires burning more strongly, cutting themselves and crying out to their gods more and more loudly. As the story continues, we read that Elijah mocked them saying, saying, "Cry aloud, for he is a god. Either he is musing, or he is relieving himself, or he is on a journey, or perhaps he is asleep and must be awakened" (v27, ESV).

I am aware this observation seems quite harsh and even condemning, but the same question arises for me – do we believe our relationship with God is hard work? Does working harder in our worship and yelling louder in our prayers make them more powerful? Do we feel as though we need to prove something about our sincerity to God, or to others, or even ourselves? Or has it just become habit?

It makes me think of the way children respond to being yelled at – generally they start to tune out. It is too much hard work to listen to. How much more powerful is a whisper or a quiet word we must stop to listen to? Further on in Elijah's story, he had an encounter where God was not in the wind, the thunder or the earthquake or the fire, but after all that stopped, He was in a whisper – the still, small voice, (1 Kings 19:11-13).

In my doubts about of some of our worship today, I might transpose that to, "He was not in the blacked-out rooms, the smoke machines, the loud drums and guitars or even the light shows", but that when we return to our closet at home, we find He was there all along. This is not to say that He can't be in these things, too, more a reflection around what space we give Him in our corporate worship times.

Another aspect of our beliefs around worship is how it might impact God. The way we seem to approach worship in most scenarios I have been involved in come from a largely unspoken or even unrecognised belief that we worship to please God, or to somehow elevate Him.

A very challenging thought I have had recently is that God actually does not need our worship. It does not change Him or how He views us. He loves us neither more nor less however we worship Him or don't.

This is quite confronting. It takes control right away from us, but it also frees us. I don't have to worship in the "right way" (however that is in our belief structure) in order for Him to deign to listen to me. I don't have to perform, or make myself somehow good enough.

From God's perspective, He is already whole, already knows who He is, and is not any better or worse off depending on our worship. It runs concurrently with the idea that God cannot experience loss. If we stop to think about this a little, we can see this is pinned on is the same issue. God is already whole and complete. He has no needs to be fulfilled.

Personally, I have come to a place of understanding that worship is more about us reminding ourselves of who God is. We worship Him to restore correct alignment in our thinking, attitudes and beliefs. God is God and I am not. He does not have to answer to me, and He certainly won't be manipulated into doing what I want. He is far more interested in what is going on in our hearts than our outward behaviour and desires.

Worship, then, for me, becomes all about positioning myself with my heart open, not only to give thanks for what He has done, but also to receive, from God, all that He has for me. In that place, I operate with far more gratitude and love for Him, which cycles into how I behave toward others. If I am in connection with God, with the Holy Trinity, then I already have all I need, and can pour out into those around me. In my interactions with the world, I can come from a place of fullness. When I live from the place of knowing that the Spirit of Christ is dwelling in me, not only can I access all the facets of the fruit of the Spirit, but I can also extend the same to everyone in my path.

There are many overlaps with these thoughts within the concept of prayer. Why do we pray and how do we pray? No one wants to spend time praying just for nothing to happen, nothing to change. What are our true expectations around prayer?

In the past, I have had people chasing me to pray for this situation or that circumstance in their lives or even further afield, their friends, family and neighbours who I don't even know.

Initially, I struggled with my response, which to be honest, in my heart was often a flat out "No!". As I unpacked what was going on for me, it comes back to all of those beliefs we have already explored here – that somehow, my prayers are more powerful than yours, that I am more spiritual in some way, so I will get the answers they seek. There is a saying that has been around for a few years now that, "there is no junior Holy Spirit", with the idea that kids can hear just as well from God as adults, and that their prayers are just as powerful. The problem is, we often don't credit adults with the same grace, as we question and judge who might have the favour of God.

As I have stepped further out of the structured church scene, I have also been deeply questioning the purpose of prayer. Perhaps some of this has come from disappointment with a number of seemingly unresolved issues we have prayed intensely about. Perhaps it is because of the failure of certain results and outworkings to manifest. However, I am also aware that so much prayer I have observed has seemed to treat God like something of a slot-machine. We pay our tithes and go through the process, hoping He will give us what we want.

A number of years back, I saw this very clearly as just another form of paganism. The underlying belief is that God is angry and mean, and we need to do certain things to get Him to do what we want. Sure, we don't sacrifice our first born anymore, and we don't make carved images to bow down before, but often our hearts are not far different. We want what we want, and we will do what it takes. I remember a discussion with a friend who was going through a difficult time. She said to me, "I don't understand why God isn't doing what I want" (or words to that effect). Before I could even think about it, the words that flew out of my mouth were, "If God just does what we want all the time, then who is God?"

Into all this mix, we also need to create some understanding of what we mean by prayer. Is it simply coming to God with our shopping list? There have been many helps I have come across over the years on how to pray. There is the ACTS model: Adoration, Confession, Thanksgiving, Supplication. There is the PUSH method: Pray Until Something Happens. We have often tied these into the idea that we need to have a devotional time every day. None of these things are bad or negative in themselves. The problem as I see it is that the underlying reason behind doing any of these is to please God. Again, nothing wrong with that, is there?

Actually, I believe there is. If we need to please God, the fundamental premise here is that God is displeased with us; we come from a starting point of experiencing His displeasure with us. A human relationship like this would quickly become abusive. Please me and you get a reward. Displease me and I will punish you.

We might not put this into words as bluntly, but our language would often suggest this is what we believe. "I am so blessed" (meaning you are not, so you must be less than); "You deserve it" (others who don't get what you have obviously don't deserve it – what made me so worthy?), and if I something bad happens to me, did I deserve that? Is it something I did, or just who I am? When we live our lives out of a place of comparison and lack, we will always find ourselves on the back foot, trying to catch up. Unfortunately, we live in a world that likes to keep us there – at the very least, it creates more sales.

As I have chased down these thoughts around worship and prayer, I have returned to the place of seeing them as the foundations of our relationship with God. I believe their role is to create an interface for us to connect with God. Worship reminds us of who God is, and postures or positions us in a place to relate to Him.

While prayer may involve asking God for stuff, I believe a "relationship around the table" kind of conversation is far more helpful and impacting. How was your day? What are you struggling with at the moment? Who are you struggling with at the moment? What is going on in your world that you would like help with? And as much as He listens to us, He longs for us to stop and create space to listen to Him. In fact, this was where I landed more recently after another worship night at a local church. The evening consisted of a couple of hours singing praise to Him, but I felt there was little to no space created to stop and listen to Him. Something was missing.

Years ago, God gave me a powerful insight into how many of us operate in prayer, and that often it is quite manipulative. It is when we make promises to God about what we will do if He will do. I watched a video recently by Joni Earekson-Tada, a woman who became quadriplegic as a teen well over fifty years ago. Over the years, she explained, she had many people pray for her to be healed in a myriad of ways. When that healing failed to manifest, blame would come. Perhaps she has some secret sin, perhaps her faith was weak, perhaps she wasn't saying the right words or she needed to fast more. While there are definitely times people are healed miraculously, there is no magic formula. If there was, we would no longer need a relationship with God.

If we view worship and prayer as spaces where we come to interact with God, how would this change our expectations of what those times are like?

Another reflection I have had around our gathering times is along the lines of the beliefs many seem to carry, that we come together for me to be reenergised. We definitely all have times when we need to be among others with like beliefs. That can be helpful to us when we are struggling. However, I do believe that many come with the expectation that the worship team will create an atmosphere to help me to worship and the pastor will give a message to encourage me, and, again, I come to receive. Recently, I heard a message on the topic of our need to meet together, and how important it is to our faith, where the speaker actually said the words, "and you come again next week to get your top up".

If we are coming to receive, coming for our top up, we become a drain on those leading. The pressure to perform for other people's expectations is exhausting, and when is it ever enough? If I don't get my top up, is it then the leader's fault? I have long asked the question, "What if we all came full and aware of our connection with God? What if we all came ready to worship and pray out of our fullness?" If we all carry the Holy Spirit in equal measure, and come from this position, imagine what the atmosphere of our worship might be like. And this leads nicely to the next chapter. Strap yourself in!

What is Church?

Embarking on a discussion about what we define as "church" seems a little fraught. There are so many lenses through which we view the structure and purpose of "church", some more helpful than others. Although there are some commonalities in what we believe about church, many of our behaviours and language would seem to suggest that what we say we believe is different to the way church manifests in our communities. I will unpack a few views as we go.

I have been involved in discussions about what church is for a number of years with a wide variety of people, including cross-culturally in Uganda. There is generally a wide level of consensus these days when we make the suggestion that church is the people, not the building. However, most are very reticent and slow to make changes to even their language, let alone behaviour and the underlying beliefs.

For well more than two decades now, in most leadership groups I have been involved with, there has been general agreement with this understanding that the church is not a building and we should not see it as such. The church is the people.

In some groups the discussion has ventured into the Greek word translated as church in most Bible translations: "ecclesia". From what I have read and heard, we could render this to mean anything from small gathering of people, to possibly a more political concept around governance of an area. Given what we know from the book of Acts, a great beginning place is the former: a smallish group of people doing life together.

This is a far cry from what we find in many places we call church today, where what is ostensibly an audience gathers while a select few perform on a stage or platform, or a place where we meet to sing a few songs and listen to someone speak before we have a cuppa and return to the rest of our lives.

I would also suggest that in many ways, church leadership has viewed the role of church being about governance, particularly about governing the "people of God". Many pastors have become people managers, making sure the flock is protected, taught right doctrine and that the church looks good to the world outside. Many church communities operate from a top-down model, with the leaders telling those below what they need to do to bring about the vision that the leader(s) have discerned as the way forward.

I do acknowledge that much of what I describe here is an oversimplification of what I observe, and that many people do have meaningful relationships within the institutional church context, both with God and each other. They are serving their neighbours and communities very well. However, this is not what I commonly observe. If it was, I believe that our wider communities would be being transformed to look more like the Kingdom of Light. There would be more love, joy, peace, patience, goodness…you get my drift. Most of us are experiencing an increase of precisely the opposite in our communities.

Digging a little deeper, into what church might look like, the Body of Christ is a frequently used term for describing followers of Jesus as a whole. This ties into Paul's writings about the many gifts given to the Body, particularly the so called "fivefold" gifts of apostle, prophet, evangelist, teacher and pastor. While I have been in a number of church communities where we have discussed these gifts and encouraged the congregation to understand how their gifts may be employed to benefit the rest of the Body, in practice generally these are utilised in a very hierarchical form. They have become titles of honour and position, often used in a way that diminishes the value of those not in those titled positions.

An example of just how unhelpful these titles have become is how we often label people "pastor" who are clearly not pastors, and generally don't do much pastoral care. Further, we often expect these "pastors" to perform any number of other tasks including leading the church, teaching and managing people and finances, again, often while not carrying these gifts. It is an aspect of church community I believe probably needs a complete overhaul.

In many smaller church communities, particularly in the Anglican (Episcopal) tradition, the expectations the congregation have of the priest (or minister) has been on the table for many decades as well. It has long been recognised that most congregation members would like to have one man (although many will allow for a woman now!), running all the activity in their church community. I remember our senior minister in a community that was experiencing reasonable growth telling me that some parishioners would be very offended if he didn't personally visit them when they were in hospital.

This illustrates another way in which some of the beliefs we have held are detrimental to us as church communities. These beliefs impact us as individuals, as well as the wider community. When we leave most of the "work" of "the church" to one or two at the top, it holds the rest of the people back from being what God is calling us to be for the world – as His Body - to be as Jesus to the world.

One of the real issues with the way we view church includes what we think the church is for. In the "I go to church every Sunday" model, complete with the over-use of the "do not forsake meeting together" card (see Heb 10:25) used to beat people up if they're not there, we still get stuck in the idea that church is somewhere I go. Whether it is like a football match, where I go to watch, or one where I play, it is still something I go to or participate in at whatever level I choose. We heard a great podcast a while back that addressed this very issue. The line that stuck with me (long after I have forgotten who the speaker was!) is, "If I go to church, then I can also leave church." Our language again exposes our beliefs and how we will behave. I am not part of the church and it is not part of me if I can leave it.

So, what is church for?

Again, we have some fundamental beliefs around our model of church that deeply impact how it functions. One of the more interesting ideas that helped me understand many institutional church operational structures relates to the way defence forces, like the army, operate.

As I understand it, there are two central operational positions within an army or, indeed, most other organisations that serve in emergencies. One is command and control; the other is mission command.

The concept of command and control means that those serving on the ground must do as they are told without question or hesitation. In a situation of life and death, or of emergency, you can understand why this would be important. You don't have time for discussion and if you are not operating as a team, it may quickly end in disaster.

On the other hand, in mission command, a team of people are released to achieve a set mission in which ever way they deem fit. They are trusted to use their skills and wisdom to get the job done without detailed instruction of what and how to do it.

Unfortunately, my experience is that many church leadership teams constantly operate out of command and control. This is exhausting and unsustainable for everyone, and gives little to no space for any autonomy or use of people's abilities to think differently and come up with better solutions. If we are cynical and look at how this worked in many armies in the past, the majority of people are simply used up as fodder to feed the (war) machine, rather than being valued what their unique gifts, abilities, viewpoints and experiences may bring.

Even if we see an alternative model of the church as a hospital, we may still be functioning from the emergency room, using command and control as an expedient method to "get the job done".

Although there are aspects of both these pictures of the church that may have merit, they still leave me with questions. If we are an army, do we actually know who or what we are fighting? Looking at the way many Christians behave, it is mostly each other, even though we might declare we are fighting evil.

Personally, fighting evil seems a little pointless. As I mentioned earlier, much evil comes from a perspective of lack. As we are told in Romans 12:21, we overcome evil with good. Doing good is probably not a descriptor many would use of much of the fighting or other behaviours Christians are seen doing in places like social media.

The picture of the church as a hospital is more appealing to me (especially as someone heavily invested in inner health). However, we must be purposeful in ensuring that people are given tools and help to move past needing the hospital, rather than viewing them as constantly needing repair.

Mostly, however we view the church as an organisation of people, we still come back to church revolving around what happens on a Sunday morning. As mentioned earlier, I went to a Sunday service a few months back where the speaker actually said the words that we needed to come to church to get a top up so we can go and serve during the week. Now, while there is some merit in that, and at times, gathering with others does energise and encourage us, if this is what we are doing, then a large proportional of what our faith is about would appear to revolve around what happens on those Sunday mornings.

This leads to another question. What is our faith about? What do we believe and what do we want out of that? Why do we believe what we believe? What's in it for me? Until we can answer these questions, we are doomed to keep going around the same hamster wheel with little to no change, especially in the community outside our four walls. It also leads me to another of topic to address.

Many Christians would hold fast to a model of Christianity based on the gospel of salvation being front and centre. The main focus of this understanding of Christianity is that "accepting Jesus as our Lord and Saviour" is what saves us from going to hell. The messaging of "if you died tonight, where would you end up?", leads to the idea that if you haven't said a prayer inviting Jesus into your heart and you die, you will end up in hell. If this is what we believe, then our whole focus is to help people not end up there. Indeed, much of the church life that I have been involved in for well over forty years has been very focussed on our role in being able to stop people going to hell for eternity.

When we look at why the church is in decline, I believe that this is a key aspect. While we tell people that all they need to do is say a prayer for the afterlife, what they do in this part of life is irrelevant. They are covered for eternity. Either that, or they live in fear that they haven't said the words right, or haven't really believed them and are still living in that place of fear. Meantime, we are teaching people that God is love, He loves us so much He died for us. However, the unspoken message is that His love must have an end date, because if we die before we accept it, we are doomed for eternity. Sorry, you missed the boat, you lose.

Within the frustration and desire for change that many Christians carry, there is an increasing call for revival. This is another Christian-ese term we use without really unpacking the meaning. In the world around us, the need for revival general comes from something dying, or being on the point of death. While I do not doubt God is doing something in the midst of these many spaces, I have to ask the question of why so many of us are constantly requiring revival? Jesus' statement in John 10:9 (AMP) suggests we already have life: "I came that they may have and enjoy life, and have it in abundance [to the full, till it overflows]." Why do we not experience and live from this promise?

I firmly believe that the only way we will experience true growth in the church is when we expand our metanarrative from simply being about some eternal life way off in the future, to something about transformation in the here and now. Tied up in the focus on after we die, is permission to abdicate any responsibility for what is going on in the communities we live in.

Further, I know numbers of people who speak out their desire for Jesus to return so they can escape from how bad the world is becoming. These types of statements fail to recognise that those desires are effectively embracing fear and powerlessness. We believe we have no influence or authority to produce any change in the communities around us. When we start to understand – through experience – that we can have greater expectations about the meaning of our own life as well as understanding our own importance in the community God has placed us in, we will engage, along with God, in the very real transformation of the world around us. But it starts with each one of us, in our internal world. In fact, a great term I recently heard is that the Kingdom is the governance of God. He is governing us, through His Holy Spirit which dwells within us. His Kingdom is here and now within us. We have the choice of what we want to do with that.

Are You Saved?

"But are you saved, brother?"

I hear these words in a deep masculine American accent. They constituted a very regular question back in the 1980s in the circles I was growing up in. It was subsequently superseded by, "Are you born again?", and those from more Pentecostal backgrounds would follow it up with, "Do you speak in tongues?" Another commonly used question from would-be-evangelists was, "If you were to die tonight, where would you go?" Even back then these questions made me feel uncomfortable when I heard them used on others. Ostensibly, those asking were concerned with the individual's eternal salvation. Unfortunately, they were more likely to make people feel judged and rejected. Do you cut the grade? Are you in or are you out? And if I choose to stay out, can we still be friends?

Although we may have softened some of our approaches to these conversations in the ensuing decades, the concept still appears to be underwritten by the assessment that people are either "in" or "out". While our desire may be that everyone would be in, we are operating from the belief that it is our personal responsibility to do our utmost to make sure of it.

I would also argue that responding to this question by saying the "sinner's prayer" doesn't necessarily create true Christians, but many who are giving lip service to a concept that often has little meaning to their lives in the here and now. I wonder if we don't use it as an expedient way of "bringing people into the Kingdom" in large volumes, as it requires minor input from those evangelising in terms of investing in longer term relationships. While this has not always been the case – some have taken the further discipling very seriously – there are many cases where, once the person is coming to church, there has been little further input and they are on their own.

This language of salvation is another example of language we have used to the point most Christians struggle to explain it. What have we been saved from? What does it mean to be born again? And would a loving God really condemn anyone to hell? (Hell is as a place of everlasting conscious torment in most definitions I have come across.) In addition, many of my friends and associates at university, back in the late 1980s, would mock Christians with the idea they were missing all the fun now. They were quite unfazed by the idea of something as remote and meaningless to them as hell after they died.

As mentioned earlier, in my earlier teen years, this sort of teaching left me with a great deal of fear. I was not alone in my friendship groups in questioning our salvation and whether we had said the prayer properly, or in an acceptable manner and were we changing enough for that to have been meaningful? We struggled to accept God's grace (we were taught way more about His wrath) and further struggled to believe that He was not more than a little bit unpredictable and grumpy. Sadly, it took me a very long time to come to a place where I no longer had that unhealthy fear of God (but that journey is another story).

Certain phrases or concepts in the Bible have been translated in ways that are quite unhelpful. Placing these alongside teaching that is also unhelpful as it has tended to centralise certain aspects of Jesus' message while ignoring others, has created an imbalance that has quite possibly led people away from a healthy relationship with God. The interpretation of salvation as only relevant to when we die has really short changed many people and once again, I would suggest is a major player in the decline of what many describe as Christianity.

A really helpful distinction I have heard more recently is around the "gospel" or "good news". Many of us have been taught that this is simply about not going to hell when we die. However, when we read the gospels, we find that Jesus talked about the Kingdom (of Heaven or of God) in the here and now a good deal. In fact, possibly the most well-known prayer in the world includes the line "Your Kingdom come, Your will be done, on earth as it is in heaven." (Matt 6:10) Why would Jesus teach us to pray something that wasn't possible?

While it is not my purpose in this book to go on a theological deep dive (especially when many more qualified have already done so), I can't help but get extremely excited when I think of Jesus' Kingdom being manifested here on earth. We don't have to live in the doom and gloom mentality of how the world is heading to certain destruction and that we are about to lose everything we hold dear. We don't have to fear the future.

Personally, I have been sitting with the idea that if God so loved the world that He gave His only Son, then He is pretty heavily invested in what happens to it. I don't think He has given up on the world, and I don't think it is a hopeless cause. And I do think that perhaps, just maybe, we, the Body of Christ, are the card up His sleeve, His secret weapon, if we just understood it.

But what does the kingdom of God manifested on earth look like? What is it evidenced by? Is it just that millions or billions of people have said "the sinner's prayer"? I really don't think so. Having connections with those in a country that is purportedly well over ninety percent Christian where corruption and exploitation are rife at every level, simply being willing to call ourselves Christian is not the answer.

To me, the Kingdom is all about love - the love that caused Jesus to lay down His life so we could live set free from those things that keep us stuck, here on earth. That love, in turn, looks very much, to me, like more joy, more peace, more patience, more kindness, more goodness, more faithfulness, more gentleness, more self-control. (Galatians 5:22-23) 1 Corinthians 13 is another great exposé on the nature and outworking of love. The concept of putting our name in place of love in those verses is a very useful insight on how we are doing. "Ruth is patient, Ruth is kind, Ruth does not…" – you get the idea.

How do we get more of this fruit, though?

Many of us have grown up with the belief that it happens by working harder at it. We must read the Bible more, pray more, fast more, gather with other believers more, worship more. If we just work harder, it will come.

When we look at the natural world, though, we see that fruit tends to come naturally, without effort, when the conditions are right. An apple tree doesn't have to work hard to make apples come. They are in its DNA. I firmly believe this is the same with the fruit of the Spirit.

But what are those conditions? John 15 is probably a great place to start. Abide in Me and I will abide in you. Again, abiding is not something we have to work at. If we believe that the Spirit of Christ dwells in us, we are already there. However, unless we believe it and live out of that place as true, we will struggle to experience it.

As I reflected on this passage a few months back, I became aware of how this scripture had so often been used in a way that was unhelpful to me. It came back to the fruit. If I don't bear fruit, I'll get cut off as a dead branch.

So often, this fruit has been presented as being about getting people saved – sharing the gospel of salvation, or doing good deeds. Are we out telling people about Jesus and bringing them to church? However, when I flip it back to the fruit of the Spirit, I get a very different perspective. By simply abiding, I will manifest the fruit of the Spirit. (And if you are now wondering just how to do that, how to abide, look out for my next book!)

A major aspect of faith that I have been enjoying much more in the last decade or so is an experiential relationship with God. What I mean by this is living from a place where I have regular encounters with Father God, Jesus and Holy Spirit through a variety of formats, be that through reading the Bible, the natural world, dreams, pictures or simply words and meaning dropping into my mind. These encounters actually bring transformation either to me or the way I view my circumstances and the world around me. At one point, something God told me to do was actually in direct opposition to what most of us have been taught…although it is probably in line with a form of fasting. He told me to do nothing.

In this period of time (which was significant), He was highlighting to me the depth to which we get our identity, sense of well-being, and worth from what we do, from the roles we play and from the validation of others through what we do.

Counter to this, He was showing me that His love was not contingent on what I did (or didn't do), that He was not more pleased with me and didn't value me more because of what I did, even (or especially) when I did it for Him. It was not an easy time. At times it is still a struggle to live from this place. The belief system that our worth and identity are intrinsically tied to what we do or how others perceive us is prevalent in most, if not all cultures on this planet. There is a constant pressure to return to conforming to the pattern of the world.

This brings us to revisit those beliefs we have deep down that continue to impact us and how we treat others. They include the very central idea that when good things happen to me, God is pleased with me, and when bad things happen, He is somehow displeased. Although very few of us may overtly say we believe this, emotionally, we often respond from this place. I would suggest that the only way we shift this response is through encounters with God, where He shows us otherwise.

This is a central understanding of how each of us can increasingly manifest the Kingdom of God. I believe that we are only able to demonstrate the fruit of the Spirit as far as we have experienced each facet from God. Starting with love, reading through 1 John, particularly chapter 4, we are told that we can only love because He first loved us, (verse 19). When Jesus gave His two commandments, He told us to love others as we love ourselves (Matt 22:39), and further, as He has loved us (John 13:34). We can only love ourselves as we have experienced ourselves as lovable and loved. This has to go way beyond intellectual assent (agreeing with it as a theoretical concept), to our lived experience.

Unfortunately, deep down many of us still believe the lie that we are not good enough and that we are unworthy of His love, and so, we fail to actually experience it. A verse which often comes to me around this thought is Romans 5:8 "But God demonstrates his own love for us in this: While we were still sinners, Christ died for us." We didn't have to do anything to be worthy.

Within all these sorts of discussions, most people always want to understand what happens to those who don't receive, who won't believe. At some level, I believe we want punishment, and I wonder if it comes back to the way in which we continue to condemn ourselves at some subliminal level? What we condemn in others is perhaps what we struggle with the most in ourselves? And what do we do with continued bad behaviour that causes not only destruction of the perpetrator, but also to those around them? How do we deal with the problem of evil?

One of the most helpful explanations I have found is the following explanation that came across my path several decades ago. It was reportedly a conversation between a university student and his mocking atheist lecturer and the definitions come from science, lending them logic.

The student asks the professor whether he believes in cold. He responds, "Of course, we all know what it is to be cold." The student replies that there is no such thing as cold. Cold is simply the absence of heat energy. He repeats the same with the word dark. No, dark does not exist, it is simply an absence of light. If we extrapolate this to evil, then, evil is simply an absence of good.

We all know that we can give darkness a great deal of power. Most of us, at least as children have had a level of fear around what we can't see when it is dark. It is quite easy to see how this correlates with Jesus' discussions about living in the Light and being Light to the world. Extending this to the fruit of the Spirit, then, as we experience God's love, joy, peace, patience, kindness, goodness, faithfulness, gentleness and self-control towards us, we can begin to extend each part to others. Where there is lack of any of this fruit in our world, we have the antidote. Why don't we use it? Probably because, at some level, we still believe we don't really deserve it, and so, we cannot receive it. (And the answer to that also comes in my next book!)

What About Hell?

Any discussion about the deconstruction of Christianity that doesn't include the issue of hell would be incomplete, as much as I don't want to make this a central facet. I don't believe it should be the main focus of our faith – let's keep that on Jesus and participating in His great and powerful love. For many, however, the concept of universalism is synonymous with deconstruction, and there is a belief that everyone who is deconstructing is a universalist. This is actually not true and once again, only leads to greater division.

For those who still aren't sure what I am talking about, let me explain. And no, I will not be clarifying exactly where I stand on this. This book is about thinking through our beliefs and going on the journey, not telling people what to believe.

In brief, however, I have to say that it was only a few years back that I actually learnt what the term "universalist" meant. At that time, it was used to describe, in derogatory terms, one of my favourite fiction authors, so, of course, I needed to understand what it was that was so bad!

For those still unsure what a universalist is, I will explain a few viewpoints around "what happens when you die" and you can decide for yourself which view is the most helpful to you in your relationship with God and in His Kingdom coming here on earth as in heaven. Hopefully, each of us can also still respect and behave respectfully to those we disagree with. After all, that is the main thing. Love one another.

Over the millenia, the concept of hell and what happens to us after we die, as taught by Church leaders, has changed a number of times, as has the view of many Christians. While I am not going to go into the theological depths of this, as there are plenty who already have, I will outline the main beliefs of what happens after we die as I perceive them.

First is the idea that hell is a place of fire God has created for those who don't accept Jesus as their Lord and Saviour within their allotted life span. It is a place you will go to for eternity, with no relief. Reform is not available.

Next on the spectrum is the idea of hell as a place of reformation, where those who have done evil get the opportunity to repent and serve sentence for their evil deeds. This is something of my understanding of the Roman Catholic concept of purgatory.

From there, we have annihilation theology. As I understand it, there are two main stances around this idea. The first is that evil doers will be completely burned up (annihilated). There is nothing left of them for eternity. The other is that all that is evil within any person, is burned up, and whatever is left is now purified for heaven, to be with God.

Finally, we have universalism. Simply put, this is the belief that Jesus has redeemed all of humanity and no one is either going to hell or being annihilated. Everyone is loved by God, and as such, is acceptable to Him.

I am aware that these are very much simplified versions of some of these beliefs, but as I mentioned earlier, it is not my purpose to go into the deep theology of this. There are plenty of authors who can explain all of this better than me. All I can suggest is that the best way to understand all these aspects is to find those who are willing to discuss all of them without casting condemnation over those who think differently. My experience and encouragement to each of us is that Jesus is with us in our journey, and He doesn't mind our questions. Rather, I think He welcomes them!

Conclusion

As I acknowledged at the beginning, this book is not about making declarations of what you should think or believe or even to try to convince you of anything. To me, that is counter-productive. More than anything, I believe the invitation from Jesus of Nazareth, who is the Christ, is to relationship and connectedness, with both the Trinity – Father, Son and Holy Spirit – and with each other. This is His desire for us and, I also believe, His desire for the whole of creation. He has designed us for connection at every level.

I am also aware that raising many of these questions can appear quite critical. I certainly do not want to be in danger of saying at any level, "Lord, I thank you that I am not like other Christians who believe…" (see Luke 18:10-12). I greatly hope that my voice here is calling us collectively to something more. I do firmly believe that the Church, the Body or Bride of Christ, has tremendous power to work with the Trinity to transform the world into the Kingdom of God. However, the manner many of us have been operating is clearly not having the effect we would like it to. It requires a major overhaul of both function and a number of mindsets for most, if not all of us!

As Jesus spoke to His followers about the way ahead, as outlined in Matthew 7, He encouraged them to ask and keep asking, seek and keep seeking, knock and keep knocking. And as we do, He further encourages us to treat others are we would like to be treated. He then urges us to take note of the fruit of those messengers who bring us information, as this will show us whether their messages are true or false.

And what is that fruit? It is our character – do we manifest love, joy, peace, patience, goodness, kindness, faithfulness, gentleness and self-control? "Against such things there is no law"…"And over all these virtues put on love, which binds them all together in perfect unity." (Gal 5:22-23; Col 3:14)

Who is Ruth Embery?

Ruth's formative church background started with the Independent Congregational model, which then turned into the Uniting Church of Australia. As a teen, her family ended up in a rural Anglican Church of the high variety (think bells, smells and sung liturgy), and she also spent time with friends in a Brethren-style congregation. As a young adult, she found herself in low Anglican Churches, and eventually in a charismatic independent church. A rather conservative suburban Baptist church followed, and most recently, a small semi-rural community church.

Alongside this wide range of experiences of what church might look like, Ruth has also been involved in a variety of leadership roles in most of them. It has not only informed her view of what church might be, but also taken her on a unique journey. Her experiences continue to expand her understanding and perception of not only what it means to be church, but also where we, the church, may be heading.

Ruth first realised she was not alone in these ideas as she completed a Master of Arts in Vocational Practice program way back in 2010. In this course, each of six semesters involved inspecting and exploring a different aspect of church life through the lens of Biblical interpretation, tradition and history. She found a freedom here to express her thoughts and explore them without the condemnation and fear so often associated with such explorations. This is a journey that has only expanded in the ensuing decade and more.

As a teacher, Ruth loves to learn, and is grateful to Jesus that He invites her on that journey with Him. With a B.Sc.Ed (Chem), Post Grad Dip Psych, MA, and a number of other proficiencies, particularly within the Inner Health realm, Ruth has a passion for helping others find freedom and wholeness through both information and experiences with Jesus. She not only heads up Voice in the Dark Publications, but also Restore Ministries.

You can find out more about Ruth, and are welcome to contact her for further discussion or questions at www.ruthembery.com.

For more books by Ruth, head over to www.voiceinthedark.org/buy-books.

Appendix

HOW DO YOU CHOOSE YOUR EXPERT?

What do you mean, how do I choose my expert? An expert is an expert, aren't they? Or are some experts more expert than others? What makes someone an expert anyway? And who chooses who gets the title "expert"?

To start with the first question, here are some options you might use in no particular order:

1. I don't choose. I allow mainstream media to choose (or tell me) who the experts are.

2. I don't choose. I allow social media to choose (or tell me) who the experts are.

3. I don't choose. I allow not-so-mainstream media to choose (or tell me) who the experts are.

4. I don't choose. I allow government officials to choose (or tell me) who the experts are (after all, they're the experts on experts, aren't they?)

5. I don't need to choose. I am the expert (armchair or otherwise).

6. I research my own experts until I find one who agrees with my opinion.

7. I research my own experts and then write a thesis examining the pros and cons of every scenario and remain sitting firmly on the fence.

Depending on your background, your understanding of experts

may range from little to no understanding to believing you have it all down pat (meanwhile not realising you actually have no idea). From my background in two wildly different sciences (Chemistry and Psychology) as well as my observations on human interactions in groups (which are pretty much anecdotal, but tell me if you disagree and haven't experienced levels of this at some point or other), I would like to unpack some of how experts get to be experts and why we should at least keep a very open mind when presented with any "expert".

One of the basic tenets of science that is not so widely publicised these days is that pretty much all science is based on assumptions. Even in good old, solid, reliable, testable, and repeat testable chemistry, THEORY is still based on ASSUMPTIONS. And if anyone tells you that we have moved on from theory to proof, in ANY AREA OF SCIENCE, dismiss them as not an expert immediately. It means they think they know everything, and therefore, they are not to be trusted.

Also, we can only DISPROVE theories. We can never prove that a theory will always stand because we haven't lived that long yet. No one knows everything, and any theory or belief about how any aspect of our universe works is only as good as the next bit of evidence that thoroughly debunks it (except when we blatantly refuse to accept that evidence until it smacks us in the face).

Which brings me to the next point.

Science does not equal fact. Science, in very basic terms, relates to the methodology of how we interpret facts/data/observations. And 99.99% of that is based on some sort of assumption at some level, particularly about whether our perspective on those facts is correct. Sometimes the assumptions are quite logical and rational. Other times not so much. Sometimes the "expert" has downright manipulated the conversation to get the result they want (aka, we don't let anyone else know the assumptions we have made). Other times we just don't want to entertain the thought that what we have been holding on to as "fact" for so long doesn't actually work, so we shut down anything that might expose us as being wrong and therefore less than.

Next point:

Nearly everyone has a bias.

Very few scientists start with a completely open mind about what they would like to find at the end of their study. This can easily impact how they interpret data, sometimes with drastic results. And is also impacted by who is paying for them to do the research.

Coming back to how we choose our experts or who gets to be one, looking at some history is helpful.

Let's head back into the nice, safe Middle Ages. One of our favourite scoffing points: "Flat earthers". Believe it or not, there was a period of time when everyone who was anyone important, who wanted to be in the "in-crowd" believed that the earth was flat. In fact, all the experts believed this and anyone who suggested otherwise could find themselves jailed if not killed. Now, of course, we all know that was because "religious nut jobs" wanted to control the masses and have power over them, and they were afraid that people wouldn't believe in God anymore if they said the earth was round. Or another way of looking at is that all these experts didn't want to lose their expert status, which, of course, was ludicrous! Why would anyone be so arrogant to behave like that over something so important?

Thank God, (or not because we threw Him out with the flat earth!), we don't think or behave like that anymore...or do we? (When was the last time you wanted to lynch a "climate change denier?"...hmmm...) Moving right along...

Let's look a bit closer to the present to something a little less controversial. The sugar-fat debate. For how many decades did experts tell us to ruthlessly expunge fat from out diet in order to lose weight? And how many people are still doing it? (And why do we continue to choose 97% fat free products with glee and dismiss full cream milk, which contains too much fat at 3%?? But sorry, I digress!)

Most people would now be aware that the advice to remove fat from our diets and replace it with sugar has led to a worldwide obesity and diabetes epidemic, not to mention the other health issues associated with losing all those fat-soluble vitamins and nutrients.

So how did these "experts" get it so wrong? A fairly plausible (and widely accepted) conspiracy theory is to do with the glut of corn syrup in the USA and some government directives as a way to shore up the economy. (If you haven't already watched The Sugar Film, it's worth checking it out.) So sorry, buddy, "Mr All-fat-must-go-expert" we have now moved you from the "in-crowd" of experts to an outcast.

Which brings me to the next point. Just how does one get chosen to be the next expert on any given topic? And what if there are differing opinions? Which one rises to the top of the heap?

This is where we get to a bit of a sticky situation. We have to go back to high school and re-examine human interactions. I have often wondered what it is about some people that as mean, nasty and spiteful as they can be, they still seem to rise to the top and be able to decide who deserves to be in and who deserves to be an outcast. If you never experienced this in your life, just watch "Mean Girls" (or perhaps reassess your own behaviour!)

Unfortunately, this doesn't end with school. If you doubt me, just have a look at how the flat earthers behaved. Only those with certain privileged knowledge or understanding, or the right connections, or the right viewpoints deserve to get a hearing. But, of course, we have evolved so far since then. We are so much more civilised and open minded these days. We'll give anyone a hearing, "the-benefit-of-the-doubt", at least for a few minutes, seconds, nanoseconds AND THEN WE'LL, what the heck, just CRUCIFY THEM ALREADY! (Don't believe me? You obviously need to get on social media more often!)

Even in the world outside social media, in my experience and observations, those who challenge or even dare to question the status quo tend to get pushed out, to not get opportunities, to not get a hearing. After all, no one likes someone who makes you feel uncomfortable or to think about things you'd rather not. (Is that a stone I see in your hand? Glad they haven't worked out how to launch them through the screen yet!). It reminds me of observations about prophets, but let's not go there right now.

And that's not to mention the difficulties of getting any evidence you might have that challenges the status quo into journals. You have to have the money to do repeated research consistently showing the same results before you have a hope of shifting anything already entrenched, and where does someone get that funding? (Big pharma connections anyone??)

So what is the answer? Can we trust anyone? Is anyone actually an expert?

If you have got this far, sorry to disappoint you, but don't ask me, I'm no expert!

However, on a serious note, we live in a time when it is getting less and less safe to have an alternative view. I'm not the first to observe that we have been pushed into a place of polarised views, and even worse, we have "omnibussed" them – if you believe (or doubt, or disagree with) X, then you automatically believe Y, Z, Q and F, even though they are completely unrelated. Added into this (which is the meaning of polarisation), if you don't believe A, then you must believe B. But I want to think about C? Is that ok? No – there are only two choices: A or B – pick a side, or we'll ostracise, ridicule and mock you mercilessly anyway.

In an age where we say we'll follow the science, and that science will give us all the answers, unfortunately we seem to have moved to the polar extreme of where science has its roots – reasoning, logic, robust discussion and thought (iron sharpens iron: those who think differently to us help us hone our own thoughts, beliefs and understanding) - and turned our brains off at the door (or other interface).

Now, do you want the red pill or the blue pill?

….Well….what do the experts say?

(PS. The emperor really isn't wearing any clothes! And if you don't know what I am talking about, just look up the story for another brilliant exposé on the experts.)

www.ingramcontent.com/pod-product-compliance
Lightning Source LLC
Chambersburg PA
CBHW071832290426
44109CB00017B/1807